❊ The ❊
PRINTERS

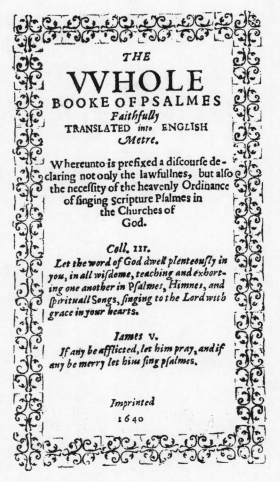

THE
VVHOLE
BOOKE OF PSALMES
Faithfully
TRANSLATED *into* ENGLISH
Metre.

Whereunto is prefixed a difcourfe de-
claring not only the lawfullnes, but alfo
the neceffity of the heavenly Ordinance
of finging Scripture Pfalmes in
the Churches of
God.

Coll. III.
*Let the word of God dwell plenteoufly in
you, in all wifdome, teaching and exhort-
ing one another in Pfalmes, Himnes, and
fpirituall Songs, finging to the Lord with
grace in your hearts.*

Iames V.
*If any be afflicted, let him pray, and if
any be merry let him fing pfalmes.*

Imprinted
1640

*Title page of the first complete book
published in the British American colonies*

COLONIAL AMERICAN CRAFTSMEN

The

PRINTERS

WRITTEN & ILLUSTRATED BY

Leonard Everett Fisher

FRANKLIN WATTS, INC.
575 Lexington Avenue, New York 22

For my children,
Julie, Susan, and James

Library of Congress Catalog Card Number: 65-12774
© Copyright 1965 by Leonard Everett Fisher
Printed in the United States of America

4 5

A Short History

"WE FIGHT NOT TO ENSLAVE, but to set a country free, and to make room upon the earth for honest men to live in."

This ringing cry for liberty was written by Thomas Paine during the American Revolution. It was printed on September 12, 1777, in a pamphlet called *The American Crisis*. The day before, General George Washington and his men had been defeated in a battle at Brandywine Creek, in Pennsylvania. Later that winter the ragged American army shivered on the frozen ground at Valley Forge.

Of all the colonial American craftsmen who used their skills to build a nation, none was as close to the spirit of liberty as was the printer. The words he printed on paper, whether they were his own or those of someone else, aroused the people with thoughts of freedom. And printed words sharpened the colonists' courage to fight on when their hopes of victory seemed dim. The printers' work in colonial America was as much a part of the fight for independence as were the

Valley Forge — the struggle for freedom

⚙ **9** ⚙

*The Reverend Jose Glover
had printing equipment
loaded aboard ship*

The *HISTORY*

bloody battles that finally drove the British from the land.

But the story of the colonial printer did not begin with the War for Independence. It started in England in 1638, when America seemed a distant, lonely, and savage place, and when the Massachusetts Bay Colony was only eight years old. In that year the Reverend Jose Glover, a Puritan clergyman, decided to help bring civilization to America. He bought a printing press, some type and ink, a large amount of paper, and other equipment, and had them loaded aboard a ship called the *John*. Together with Stephen Daye, who was a locksmith hired to accompany him, and with their two families, Mr. Glover embarked for America. But he never arrived there. He died at sea.

Stephen Daye completed the journey, however. When the *John* reached America, Mrs. Glover put Stephen Daye in charge of the press and its printing. A house was provided for the Dayes in the tiny Puritan settlement of Cambridge, on the banks of the Charles River, just west of Boston. There Stephen Daye, with the

help of his son Matthew, set up the first printing press in the British American colonies. Cambridge, the home of Harvard College, was a place of ideas, and a good location for a printing press.

But Stephen Daye could not print just anything he pleased. He operated his press by special permission granted by the government of the Massachusetts Bay Colony. And that colony was ruled, in turn, by England. If the government did not like what Daye printed it could take away his license. He would then be unable to go on printing.

The church authorities also had a great deal to say about what Stephen Daye could print. They provided much of the work for him. If the church pastors did not approve of what was being printed, they could simply stop sending work to the press. If that were to happen, Stephen Daye would lose business.

And so it happened that the first thing printed in British America on the Daye press was "The Free-man's Oath," a statement of allegiance which citizens must agree to. This was printed in 1639. Another of the early works of the press was for

the church. It was *The Whole Booke of Psalmes,* now often known as the "Bay Psalm Book." It appeared in 1640, and was the first full-length book published in the British colonies of America.

The *HISTORY*

In 1649, Samuel Green became the printer at the press, and Stephen Daye went into another business. In 1660, Green started to print a work for the Reverend John Eliot, a missionary to the Indians. It was a translation of the English Bible into the language of the native Algonquins. Samuel Green was later helped by Marmaduke Johnson, and the work was finished in 1663.

Marmaduke Johnson was not content to work under the watchful eye of another person, however. In 1665 he bought a press and type of his own. Against the wishes of the church officials, he asked for government permission to set up a press in Boston. After some trouble, he received permission and went about establishing his press across the Charles River. Unfortunately, he died before he could start operating it. Nevertheless, by refusing to surrender his right to print what and where he pleased, Johnson supported the idea that in America the printers should be free to decide about their work for themselves.

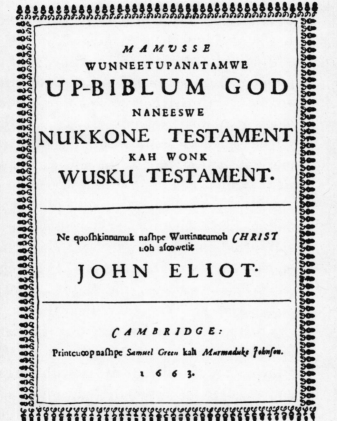

MAMUSSE
WUNNEETUPANATAMWE
UP-BIBLUM GOD
NANEESWE
NUKKONE TESTAMENT
KAH WONK
WUSKU TESTAMENT.

Ne quoſhkinnumuk naſhpe Wuttinneumoh *CHRIST*
ι.oh aſoowetit

JOHN ELIOT·

CAMBRIDGE:
Printcuωop naſhpe *Samuel Green* kah *Marmaduke Johnſon.*
1 6 6 3.

Front page of the
New-York Gazette *for the week*
of November 28, 1726

Some years later, another printer dared to be critical of church authorities. He was William Bradford of Philadelphia, Pennsylvania.

Bradford had come to America with an early group of Quakers. In 1685, three years after his arrival on Pennsylvania soil, he started Philadelphia's first printing press.

The Quakers feared that printers were troublemakers. Yet Bradford was permitted to work for eight years. Then in 1693 he wrote and printed a series of pamphlets which some of the Quakers did not like. They brought him to a court trial, and forced him to move to New York. He went on with his work there, and in 1725 founded the city's first newspaper, the *New-York Gazette.*

The *New-York Gazette* was not British America's first newspaper. The very first one was *Publick Occurrences*, printed in Boston in 1690. It criticized the British in their war with the French, and so after one issue the paper was quickly stopped by the government. It had no license, anyway, so stopping it was an easy matter.

Nevertheless, the people of Boston were determined to have a better way of learning the latest

The S P E E C H *of the Honourable* Patrick Gordon Efq; *Lieut. Governour of the Province of Pennfylvania, and Counties of* New-Caftle, Kent & Suffex, *upon Delaware.*

To the Reprefentatives of the Freemen of the faid Province of *Pennfylvania,* November 22*d.* 1726.

Mr. Speaker, and Gentlemen of the Houfe of Reprefentatives;

HAVING fully declared to the laft Affembly, what I take to be incumbent on me, in the Difcharge of my Truft; I fhall now recommend to you fuch Matters relating to the Publick, as may be proper for your Confideration.

And in the firft Place our Bills of Credit will claim your Regard: At your firft Meeting in *October,* I acquainted you with a Letter, I had received but two Days before, from the Secretary to the Right Honourable the Lords Commiffioners for Trade and Plantations, on the Subject of our *Paper-Currency,* which I now lay before you. By this Letter you will obferve what Impreffions the Conduct of fome of thefe *American* Colonies had made on that Board, to the Difadvantage of fuch Bills: Yet notwithftanding their Diflike to them in general, They have exprefs'd fo much Tendernefs for the People of this Province, who have now that *Currency* in their Hands, that we may, I hope, juftly conclude the former Acts for eftablifhing it are happily out of Danger of a Repeal. But as the Act paft laft Year, for the re-emitting part of the fame Bills out of the Loan-Office, may be thought to interfere with their Lordfhips Directions; it will require our ferious Application, to find out proper Meafures for fecuring this equally with the other Acts; which 'tis hoped may be fuccefsfully effected, when their Lordfhips are duly apprized, that the Trade between *Britain* and this Province has been fo far from Suffering, that it has been manifeftly encreafed fince the Eftablifhment of that *Currency* here; and that more *Britifh Goods* have been imported, more Ships Built in this Place for their Merchants, than had been for many Years before: But more efpecially that this *Currency* inftead of finking in Value, which has been the great and chief Objection to it in fome other Colonies, now actually rifes with us, being at this Time at lefs than half the Difcount, that, as I have

been affured, it bore with Gold and Silver, but a few Months before my Arrival. When this is July reprefented to their Lordfhips, I hope we fhall have no Room to doubt, but they will abate in their Opinions of the ill Confequences of that *Currency,* efpecially in this Colony: And therefore feeing *Ten Thoufand Pounds* of the Bills now in the People's Hands, fubfift on the Foundation of the laft Act, which was paft before their Lordfhips Sentiment were made known to us, we may hope for their Indulgence to that alfo. To obtain which I fhall very heartily joyn with you Gentlemen, in whatever fhall be reafonably propofed.

I cannot but with great Pleafure take Notice on this Occafion, of the happy Profpect that this Province now affords, of fupplying, by the Induftry of it's Inhabitants, the want of thofe natural Advantages, that have attended divers of the *American* Colonies (in making Returns with their own Product directly for *Britain*) which in all Probability muft in due time introduce real Wealth, and a *Currency* of intrinfic Value amongft us. Several Companies are already engaged in carrying on *Iron Works. Hemp,* from the Incouragement given, I am told, is raifed in much greater Quantities; But the firft of thefe requiring a large Stock, and the other very fertile or enriched Land, which may difable poorer Families from partaking of their Benefits, Providence feems now to have pointed out one Method more, for Imploying even the mean and weak, as well as others of both Sexes, to confiderable Advantage, by raifing *Silk;* which (as I am credibly informed) is produced here, as fine and good, as moft the World affords, and with as much Eafe: Thefe three are Commodities for which *Britain* pays dear to other Countries, and with which there can be no Danger of overftocking the Market: therefore as nothing can be more acceptable to *Britain,* than to receive from it's own Colonies, what it purchafes more difadvantagetoufly from Foreigners, nothing perhaps may better deferve the Notice and Encouragement of the Legiflature.

Thefe, *Gentlemen,* are the Heads I fhall at prefent mention: What further occurs may be fent to you by Meffages. I fhall only here obferve that from the Views I have yet had of this Province; it appears very plain, that we are, or may be, a very happy People; if we can but act worthy of thofe Bleffings, which feem to have
attended

Front page of the
New-England Courant *for the week*
of February 4, 1723

happenings than by listening to the voice of the town crier or the town gossip. They wanted a newspaper. In 1704, John Campbell, the postmaster of Boston, started the *Boston News-Letter.*

Fifteen years later, the *American Weekly Mercury* was founded in Philadelphia by Andrew Bradford, the son of William Bradford. In 1721, Boston had another newspaper, the *New-England Courant.* It was printed by James Franklin, older brother of Benjamin Franklin.

James Franklin began teaching the craft of printing to twelve-year-old Benjamin in 1718. By 1721, Benjamin was not only a skilled printer; he was also a talented writer. Unknown to his older brother, and using the name of "Mrs. Silence Dogood," fifteen-year-old Benjamin wrote various articles for the paper. The pieces were bright and sharp and original, and more people bought the paper because of them.

But Benjamin Franklin did not take kindly to being ordered about by his brother. In 1723, at the age of seventeen, he went to Philadelphia. There, in 1730, he purchased his own printing shop. From his press came *Poor Richard's Al-*

The *HISTORY*

THE
New-England Courant.

From MONDAY February 4. to MONDAY February 11. 1723.

The late Publisher of this Paper, finding so many Inconveniencies would arise by his carrying the Manuscripts and publick News to be supervis'd by the Secretary, as to render his carrying it on unprofitable, has intirely dropt the Undertaking. The present Publisher having receiv'd the following Piece, desires the Readers to accept of it as a Preface to what they may hereafter meet with in this Paper.

Non ego mordaci distrinxi Carmine quenquam,
Nulla venenato Litera mista Joco est.

LONG has the Press groaned in bringing forth an hateful, but numerous Brood of Party Pamphlets, malicious Scribbles, and Billingsgate Ribaldry. The Rancour and bitterness it has unhappily infused into Mens minds, and to what a Degree it has sowred and leaven'd the Tempers of Persons formerly esteemed some of the most sweet and affable, is too well known here, to need any further Proof or Representation of the Matter.

No generous and impartial Person then can blame the present Undertaking, which is designed purely for the Diversion and Merriment of the Reader. Pieces of Pleasancy and Mirth have a secret Charm in them to allay the Heats and Tumors of our Spirits, and to make a Man forget his restless Resentments. They have a strange Power to tune the harsh Disorders of the Soul, and reduce us to a serene and placid State of Mind.

The main Design of this Weekly Paper will be to entertain the Town with the most comical and diverting Incidents of Humane Life, which in so large a Place as Boston, will not fail of a universal Exemplification: Nor shall we be wanting to fill up these Papers with a grateful Interspersion of more serious Morals, which may be drawn from the most ludicrous and odd Parts of Life.

As for the Author, that is the next Question. But tho' we profess our selves ready to oblige the ingenious and courteous Reader with most Sorts of Intelligence, yet here we beg a Reserve. Nor will it be of any Manner of Advantage either to them or to the Writers, that their Names should be published; and therefore in this Matter we desire the Favour of you to suffer us to hold our Tongues: Which tho' at this Time of Day it may sound like a very uncommon Request, yet it proceeds from the very Hearts of your Humble Servants.

By this Time the Reader perceives that more than one are engaged in the present Undertaking. Yet is there one Person, an Inhabitant of this Town of Boston, whom we honour as a Doctor in the Chair, or a perpetual Dictator.

The Society had design'd to present the Publick with his Effigies, but that the Limner, to whom he was presented for a Draught of his Countenance, descryed (and this he is ready to offer upon Oath) Nineteen Features in his Face, more than ever he beheld in any Humane Visage before; which so raised the Price of his Picture, that one Master himself forbid the Extravagance of coming up to it. And then besides, the Limner objected a Schism in his Face, which splits it from his Forehead to a

strait Line down to his Chin, in such sort, that Mr. Painter protests it is a double Face, and he'll have Four Pounds for the Pourtraiture. However, tho' this double Face has spoilt us of a pretty Picture, yet we all rejoiced to see old Janus in our Company.

There is no Man in Boston better qualified than old Janus for a Couranteer, or if you please, an Observator, being a Man of such remarkable Opticks, as to look two ways at once.

As for his Morals, he is a chearly Christian, as the Country Phrase expresses it. A Man of good Temper, courteous Deportment, sound Judgment; a mortal Hater of Nonsense, Foppery, Formality, and endless Ceremony.

As for his Club, they aim at no greater Happiness or Honour, than the Publick be made to know, that it is the utmost of their Ambition to attend upon and do all imaginable good Offices to good Old Janus the Couranteer, who is and always will be the Readers humble Servant.

P.S. Gentle Readers, we design never to let a Paper pass without a Latin Motto if we can possibly pick one up, which carries a Charm in it to the Vulgar, and the learned admire the pleasure of Construing. We should have obliged the World with a Greek scrap or two, but the Printer has no Types, and therefore we intreat the candid Reader not to impute the defect to our Ignorance, for our Doctor can say all the Greek Letters by heart.

His Majesty's Speech to the Parliament, October 11. tho' already publish'd, may perhaps be new to many of our Country Readers ; we shall therefore insert it in this Day's Paper.

His MAJESTY's most Gracious SPEECH to both Houses of Parliament, on Thursday October 11. 1722.

My Lords and Gentlemen,

I Am sorry to find my self obliged, at the Opening of this Parliament, to acquaint you, That a dangerous Conspiracy has been for some time formed, and is still carrying on against my Person and Government, in Favour of a Popish Pretender.

The Discoveries I have made here, the Informations I have received from my Ministers abroad, and the Intelligences I have had from the Powers in Alliance with me, and indeed from most parts of Europe, have given me most ample and current Proofs of this wicked Design.

The Conspirators have, by their Emissaries, made the strongest Instances for Assistance from Foreign Powers, but were disappointed in their Expectations: However, confiding in their Numbers, and not discouraged by their former ill Success, they resolved once more, upon their own strength, to attempt the subversion of my Government.

To this End they provided considerable Sums of Money, engaged great Numbers of Officers from abroad, secured large Quantities of Arms and Ammunition, and thought themselves in such Readiness, that had not the Conspiracy been timely discovered, we should, without doubt, before now have seen the whole Nation, and particularly the City of London, involved in Blood and Confusion.

The Care I have taken has, by the Blessing of God, hitherto prevented the Execution of their traiterous Projects. The Troops have been incamped all this Summer; six Regiments (though very necessary for the Security of that Kingdom) have been brought over from Ireland; The States General have given me assurances that they would keep a considerable Body of Forces in readiness to go back on the first No-

Front page of the
Pennsylvania Gazette *for the week*
of October 22, 1730

The *HISTORY*

manack, and a newspaper, the *Pennsylvania Gazette.* And from his shop came a famous patriot, diplomat, scientist, inventor, author, and thinker — one of America's great men, who wrote of himself as "I, Benjamin Franklin, Printer. . . ."

Perhaps Benjamin Franklin, in wanting to be known first and foremost as a printer, was anxious for people to know of his humble beginnings. Perhaps, in calling attention to the fact that he was a printer, Benjamin Franklin was voicing his belief in the power of the printed word to move men's minds to do good or evil. Whatever the reason, he certainly knew that one of the first battles for freedom waged between Britain and America centered around a printer and his press. The printer was John Peter Zenger, editor of the *New-York Weekly Journal.*

Zenger was arrested by the British in 1735 for printing articles that criticized the colonial governor. The law was clear in this matter, and Zenger had broken it. Andrew Hamilton, the lawyer who defended Zenger, argued at the trial, however, that Zenger had merely printed the truth. He said that the jury should be allowed to con-

THE
Pennfylvania *GAZETTE*.

Containing the frefheft Advices Foreign and Domeftick.

From Thurfday, October 22. to Thurfday, October 29. 1730.

The SPEECH of the HONOURABLE

Patrick Gordon, Efq;

Lieutenant Governor of the Counties of *New-Caftle*, *Kent* and *Suffex* on *Delaware*, and Province of *Pennfylvania*.

To the Reprefentatives *of the faid Counties in* General Affembly *met, at* New-Caftle, *the 21ft of* October, 1730.

GENTLEMEN,

MY fteady Endeavours to put in Practice as well his late facred Majefty's Commands to Me, which I mentioned at My firft Arrival here, as My Inftructions from our Honourable Proprietors, together with the happy Concurrence of the People in joining with what they manifeftly faw was aimed folely at their own Good, have by Divine Providence been bleffed with fuch Succefs, that now on Our annual Meeting, there feems little more Incumbent on Me, than to exprefs My Satisfaction in the Opportunity given Me of feeing the Reprefentatives of His Majefty's good Subjects under my Care, convened together; and I hope it proves no lefs agreeable to You, GENTLEMEN, to have the fame on Your Parts of meeting Me; that We may between Us fhew that mutual Harmony, which will ever be the happy Refult of a Difpofition in thofe concerned in the Affairs of Our Government, to difcharge their refpective Duties with Loyalty to His Majefty, Fidelity to Our Proprietors, and with Benevolence and Affection in every Individual towards his Neighbour.

The Continuance of this, GENTLEMEN, I heartily recommend to You, and that if Particulars fhould yet harbour any Mifunderftandings or private Uneafineffes, they fhould, from a View of the Lovelinefs of Peace and publick Tranquility, entirely lay them afide, that We may truly appear to all, what I think We really are, as happy a People among Ourfelves, as any in His Majefty's Dominions.

GENTLEMEN,

You will now undoubtedly of Courfe, at this Meeting, take into Confideration what yet remains from former Affemblies to be compleated or regulated; and herein, I hope, You will fhew fuch Unanimity, and make fuch Difpatch, as will fully prove We are all fenfible of the Bleffings we enjoy; and on My Part, nothing fhall be wanting to improve them.

P. GORDON.

To the HONOURABLE

Patrick Gordon, Efq;

Lieutenant Governor of the Counties of *New-Caftle*, *Kent* and *Suffex* on *Delaware*, and Province of *Pennfylvania*.

The Humble ADDRESS of the Reprefentatives *of the Freemen of the faid Counties, in* General Affembly *met, at* New-Caftle *the 22d of* October, 1730.

May it pleafe Your HONOUR,

WE, *the Reprefentatives of thefe Counties, do with the greateft Senfe of Gratitude, return Our fincere Thanks for Your favourable and kind Speech to Us ; and We are extreamly pleafed that there appears to Your Honour fo happy a Difpofition amongft the People whom We reprefent, of Peace and Harmony, as that you do not find it neceffary upon this Occafion to to do more than exprefs Your Satisfaction in meeting Us at this Time ; which next to the Divine Providence arifes from the happy Effects of Your Honour's mild and prudent Adminiftration ; and we fhould be wanting to Ourfelves, as well as Our Conftituents, fhould We on Our Parts lofe any Opportunity of improving or maintaining the fame : We fhall at all Times endeavour to difcharge Ourfelves with Duty and Loyalty to His Majefty, Affection and all due Refpect to Your Honour, and Fidelity to Our Proprietor.*

It is a Bleffing greatly to be valued, that there are not any Difcontents or Mifunderftandings remaining

Front page of the
New-York Weekly Journal *for the*
week of April 7, 1735

The *HISTORY*

sider not just whether Zenger had broken the law, but whether truth or falsehood had been printed. This was against the judge's wishes, but the jury agreed, and Zenger was set free.

Zenger's trial resulted in a famous victory for the idea that a printer should be free to print the facts, however unpleasant they might be to some people. From that day on and for the next forty years, England had to suffer the attacks on her authority made by furious colonists and their printing presses — printing what they felt to be the truth. Ꮬ

Numb. LXXIV

THE

New - York Weekly JOURNAL

Containing the freſheſt Advices, Foreign, and Domeſtick.

MUNDAY April 7th, 1735.

Sir.

IN my former I ſhewed, that allowing all that Mr. *Murray* wanted to prove, *viz.* That the Juriſdiction of the great Courts of *England* extend to *New-York*, the preſent ſupream Court of *New-York*, cannot exiſt lawfully, and exerciſe the ſame Powers which thoſe Courts have ; and I now further add, that no Ordinance of the Governor & Council, or even Act of the Legiſlature of this Province can give it the ſame Powers ; becauſe that cannot be done without deſtroying the Powers of the great Court of *England*, ſo far at leaſt as relates to this Province : For, *as* I obſerved, both cannot have the ſame Powers at the ſame Time and in the ſame Place, and the Legiſlature of this province has no Kind of Authority over the great Courts or any Courts in *England*.

Mr. *Murray* in ſome Part of his Opinion, ſays, that the Argument which proves too much proves nothing. And I ſay, when a Concluſion evidently falſe is drawn, it ſhews one or more of the Propoſitions from whence it is deducted are falſe, and that the Arguer has made a Slip in the Deduction : For from Truth Truth always follows, and Truth never brings forth Falſhood. For this Reaſon its to examine Mr. *Murray*'s Propoſitions.

The Firſt is, that the Great Courts in *England* are Fundamental Courts, and this muſt be with Reſpect to the Conſtitution : For if it be taken in any other Senſe, the Concluſion which he draws from it will not follow. The Word Fundamental comes from Foundation ; ſo that when we ſay any Thing is Fundamental of another we ſay, that that Thing is the Foundation where on the other is built, and if we conceive that the Thing which is the Foundation be taken away we imediately perceive that the other Thing which is built upon it muſt tumble down, and fall to Pieces. Now I preſume that any Man may eaſily conceive how any one or all of the Courts in *England* may be diſſolved, and other Courts Eſtabliſhed in their Room, without the leaſt Injury to the Conſtitution ; and therefore I conclude, that theſe Courts are not Fundamental to the Conſtitution, as Mr. *Murray* ſuppoſes, but that his firſt fundamental Propoſition is falſe, and therefoe that all his Arguments built upon it muſt fall to the Ground- Its ſo eaſie to conceive, how theſe Courts may be diſſolved, without injury to the Conſtitution, and others eſtabliſhed, that Mr. *Murray* would think me idle if I would take up Time to ſhew it. But to put it beyond Contradiction, and any Gentleman's Skill in Sophiſtry to perſwade any Man of Senſe, that the great Courts are Fundamental, that is ſuch without which our Conſtitution can't exiſt, we need only obſerve, that there are many Places in *England* which

How the
Printers Worked

A PRINTER'S TOOLS

Inking pad

Type

Composing stick

PRINTING IS A MEANS OF PRESSING letters, words, sentences, and pictures onto a sheet of paper.

In order to do his work, the printer must have certain equipment. Chief among it are three things: metal type, ink, and a printing press.

The colonial printer's *type* was made up of a great number of single metal letters of the alphabet. They could be put together to make words and sentences, which could then be combined into pages. Once each page of type was inked, it could be printed in as many copies as were needed. Then the single metal letters could be separated. They could be used again and again, to make many different words and sentences and pages. They were called *movable* type, because the single letters could be moved about to make a variety of words.

John Gutenberg seems to have been the first man to work out practical ways of making type and putting it together with ink and a press to do a satisfactory job of printing. He did his work in Germany between the 1440's and the 1460's —

Compositor   Making up a form

Cleaning a form   *Printing*   *A colonial printing shop*

❈ 27 ❈

about two hundred years before Stephen Daye printed *The Whole Booke of Psalmes.*

A complete collection of all the type characters in the same size and style was called a *font.* It contained greater quantities of some letters than of others, because the printer would use more of them. He would use more E's than X's, for example. A printer bought as many type fonts as he might need or could afford.

Each piece of type had to be made in a special metal-working shop called a *type foundry.* There were no type foundries in British America in the early days. Nearly every piece of type used by the colonial American printers had to be imported from across the sea.

The early American printer was a man of many talents. He was a *writer.* He printed not only the written works of other people, but his own work as well. He was also an *editor,* a person who prepared and corrected the work at hand. He was a *publisher,* a person who issued printed material for sale. He was a *compositor,* a man who arranged the type letters into words, the words into sentences, and the sentences into

The *TECHNIQUE*

Hammer

Counterpunch

1. STAMPING

Heat-softened steel punch,
holding shape of letter D

Vise

2. FILING

Steel punch

File

3. PUNCHING

Steel punch

Copper matrix

Vise

Molten metal poured into
slot and down onto matrix

4. CASTING

Type mold

Matrix, with tab for removing
type for letter D from mold

Clamp

pages. And he was a *pressman,* a person who operated a press.

If his printing shop was a large one, the printer employed skilled helpers to do some of these jobs. And he hired young *apprentices,* called *devils,* to work while at the same time they learned the printing craft. But if his shop was a small one, the printer did most of the work himself.

However large or small the shop might be, after the type arrived the next job belonged to the compositor. He placed the single pieces of type in a specially built shallow tray called a *case.* It was only an inch deep and was divided into two main sections. The upper section contained all the capital letters. Each kind of letter was put into a smaller section of its own, within the upper case — the K's in one little section, the W's in another, and so on. Thus, because of their location in the case, capital letters are still sometimes known as *upper case* letters.

The small letters were placed in their individual sections in the lower case. Hence these small letters are still known as *lower case* letters.

The letters were not arranged alphabetically,

A B C D E F G
H I K L M N O
P Q R S T V X
â ê î ô û Y Z
á í ó ú ; ſb
à è ì ò ù
* ꝏ J U j ſt ſſ

A B C D E F G
H I K L M N O
P Q R S T V X
J U Æ æ § Y Z
ffl ë Œ œ † [ ] !
fl ï W w ( ) ?
ff Ç ç É é ”

° ç é - , ,
& b c d e
z
y 1 m n i
x v u t ſpaces

1 2 3 4 5 6 7 8
s f f g h 9 0
æ œ
ffi ffl k en quads
o p q fi fl : quads
a r . , em quads

❁31❁

but for convenience. The characters that would be used the most were placed nearest at hand. A beginning compositor's first job was to "learn the case" — learn the location of the letters so that he could reach for them without even looking.

The TECHNIQUE

When the compositor was ready to arrange, or *set*, the letters into words, he tacked the handwritten sheet of paper that he was to follow onto a reading stand fastened to the case. This handwritten sheet was called *copy*. Standing before the tilted type case and without taking his eyes off the copy, the compositor chose the proper letters and slid them one by one into a small, flat frame called a *composing stick*, which he held in his other hand.

When he had finished placing a single line in the stick, he spaced the letters and words out with slivers of brass so that the line would reach an exact measured length. Then he went on to the next line of type. When the composing stick was filled with lines all the same length, he removed them to a metal pan called a *galley*.

When the compositor had filled the galley with enough type to make one printed page, it was

Tapping the type in the form.
The man in background
holds a made-up form of type

inked and a rough print or *proof* was made of it. This *galley proof* was used to make any corrections or changes before the final printing.

The *TECHNIQUE*

After all the pages to be printed had been corrected, the set type was transferred from the galleys to a large, perfectly flat and smooth slab of *stone.* There the type was put into a large metal frame, or *chase,* and was locked in place so tightly that it could not fall out. Sometimes the printer locked up one page, sometimes two pages, but rarely more than four pages. It all depended on the job being done, and the size of the press. The pages locked into the chase were called the *form.*

Next, the printer lightly tapped the form with a flat piece of wood, to make the surface of the letters as level as possible. When this had been done, the form was ready for the press.

The early printing presses were wooden machines that stood a foot or two taller than a man. Running through the upright supports was a waist-high, table-like frame called a *carriage.* On the carriage was a wooden plank that slid back and forth along two rails. Fastened on top of the plank was another frame called a *coffin.*

The *TECHNIQUE*

Hinged to the coffin was the *tympan,* two tightly fitted frames over which was stretched parchment, much like that on a drum. The tympan held a soft padding useful in keeping the type from breaking under pressure when the paper was finally pressed against it. Another light frame was hinged to the tympan. It was called a *frisket.*

The printer placed the form in the coffin of the press. There, by means of two leather balls, he carefully inked the type. He then placed a sheet of paper on the tympan and folded the frisket over it, to hold it in place. The paper had been dampened in order to make sure that when it was pressed against the type it would lie flat and every inked piece of type would touch it.

The frisket and the tympan were again folded over. Now the paper that they held rested above the inked form in the coffin. The coffin was then slid along the carriage rails until it was directly under a four-inch-thick piece of hardwood called the *platen.*

The platen was attached to the bottom of a large *screw,* which in turn hung from a crossbar called the *head.* About halfway between the

Cap (crossbar)

Head (crossbar)

Cheek (upright)

Screw

Hose

Lever bar

Till (crossbar)

Platen

Frisket

Tympan

Coffin

Plank

Rails

Carriage

Cheek (upright)

Ink pad

LEF

Spit handle (turns spit that rolls coffin under platen)

❖ 37 ❖

head and the platen was another crossbar called
the *till*. The screw, enclosed in a box called a *hose,*
passed through the till.

The *TECHNIQUE*

When all was ready, the printer put a bar into
the screw and worked it down so that it pressed
the platen onto the coffin. This pressure held the
paper against the inked type. When the type letters had been printed on the paper, the platen
was raised. Then the coffin, with the form, was
rolled back to the end of the carriage. Here the
frisket and the tympan were folded back, and
the printed page was removed to a place where it
could dry.

This process was repeated until the printer
had as many copies or *impressions* of the page as
were needed. Then the form was removed from
the coffin and was washed with a solution of
alkali. This alkali cut through the ink's thick·
substance and left the type clean. All the type
pieces that made up the form were then returned
to their proper places in the type case, to be used
again later.

The colonial printer's method of printing a page
was called *letterpress*. That is to say, it was a
method by which a flat sheet of paper was pressed

Front page of the
Boston News-Letter *for the week*
of May 15, 1704

against a surface of raised letters that had been inked. This method, much modernized, is still used today in some forms of printing, and is still called *letterpress.*

The *TECHNIQUE*

The sturdy wooden presses used by the colonial printers were *sheet-fed, flat-bed* presses. That is, the printers placed paper, a sheet at a time, on a press which held the type in a flat, horizontal frame, or *bed.*

Some of these early printing presses were so strongly built that they were in continuous use for more than one hundred years. It should be remembered, however, that the presses used by the colonial printers were all made in Europe. It was not until some years after the Revolutionary War that Americans began to make their own presses.

Importing most of their tools and materials was bothersome to the colonial printers, but they made the best of it. Their real concern was for their product. And their product was printed words. They made sure that the paper, type, ink, and presses they used were the best they could get, so that the words and ideas they printed could be clearly and easily read by the people. ᧥

The Boston News-Letter.

Published by Authority.

From Monday May 15. to Monday May 22. 1704.

Westminster, Novemb. 12. 1703.
The Address of the Lords Spiritual and Temporal, presented Her Majesty.

WEE Your Majesties most dutiful and loyal Subjects, the Lords Spiritual and Temporal in Parliament Assembled, do offer up our hearty acknowledgments to Almighty God, for the preservation of Your Royal Person, so essential to the happiness of Your People, & the Safety of *Europe*.

We see, with the greatest satisfaction, the zeal with which Your Majesty espouses the Publick Interest, which carries You even beyond the obligations of Your Treaties in Defence of the House of *Austria*, against the Usurpations of the House of *Bourbon*, & the glorious restitution of that Family to the Monarchy of *Spain*, which we have great reason to expect from the late Alliance with the King of *Portugal*, will be chiefly owing to Your Majesties Arms and Assistance.

Your Majesty may depend upon Security at home in the love of Your People, our Persons & Fortunes shall ever be ready to defend You upon all occasions, and Your Majesty may therefore, with the greater Safety and Glory, send Your Fleets and Armies abroad in the Defence of Your Allies.

The happy Declaration of the Duke of *Savoy*, for the common Interest, gives Your Majesty a seasonable opportunity to shew Your Compassion and concern for those Protestants in the South of *France*, who lie under the heaviest Persecution and oppression.

We lament for our selves and others the unavoidable expences of War, but have reason to thank God and Your Majesty, that we are free from all the other Calamities of it, having almost nothing else to wish for (being secured of a Protestant Succession) but Your long and happy Reign over us: And we shall most willingly pay our proportion Taxes, encouraged by Your Royal Generosity for the ease of Your People, & by the frugal management of what is given; being sensible, there is no better way to save the Wealth of the Nation, than by carrying on the War at this time with the utmost vigour.

Your Majesty may expect from us a most ready compliance with all Your desires, so justly merited by Your care of the general welfare and happiness of Your People, extended even to the poorest and meanest of Your Subjects.

This appears yet more eminently in that earnest and pressing Recommendation to Your Parliament of Union and Peace amongst themselves; And we, in the most solemn manner, Assure Your Majesty, That we will not only avoid, but oppose whatsoever may tend to create any disquiet or disunion amongst Your Subjects.

We shall never be wanting in any part of our Duty towards the Supporting Your Majesties honour & Your Allies, not doubting but Almighty God will prosper Your Majesties Arms, so gloriously employed to protect all those whom the ambition of the *French* King would oppress.

To which Her Majesty return'd Her most Gracious Answer in these words.

My Lords,

I Am extreamly sensible of the particular concern You express for me in this Address, and of Your great zeal for the common cause of *Europe*.

I rely very much upon the Assurances You give me of Your Duty and Affection, and shall always use my best endeavours to establish the safety and happiness of the Kingdom.

Piscataqua, May, 13. Letters thence acquaint us of some more damage, done by the Sculking Adversary, on the 11. instant *Nicholas Cole* of *Wells*, with *Nicholas Hogden, Thomas Dane* and *Benjamin Gough*, Souldiers, went about a Mile from Capt. *Wheelwright's* Garrison to Look after his Cattle and on their return were Attack't by 12. Indians, who kill'd said *Cole* and *Hogden*, took *Dane* Captive, *Gough* escaping, advised Capt. *Hales* of it, who immediately called his Souldiers together; but the Enemy were fled.

Her Majesties Council by His Excy. direction hath appointed Thursday the 18. instant a day of Publick Fasting with Prayer, being the same day appointed by His Excy. & Council in the Province of *Mass.Bay* and for said ends contain'd in said Proclamation.

Arrived here *John Holcom* from *Antigua, Richard Shortridge* for *Fyall* wind-bound. Outward-bound, Capt. *Alcock* for *Barbados* ready to Sail, *John Pratt* for said Port in Ten days, and *Robert Emery* in about 3 weeks, and *Richard Waterhouse* for St. Christophers in a Week.

Northampton, May 13. A Company of Indians and French, between day break and Sun-rising, about 60 Set upon a Garrison-house of *Benj. Jones's*, about two Miles from the body of the Town, and set fire to it ere they were aware of it; Kill'd and carryed Captive about 30. Persons. The Town being Alarmed, pursued them, the Enemy finding it, scattered themselves into parties; and so did the English into Ten in a Company, pursuing them; Capt. *Taylor* was kill'd in the pursuit.

Lisbon, March 27. On the advice brought the King of *Portugal*, of the Fleet from *England*, being on the Coast in whom was the King of *Spain*; he ordered a Wharff to be made from his Palace to the Waterside, & overlaid it with Cloath of Scarlet, and went in his Barge on board to receive him, returned and the King of *Spain* on his right hand ; who was received with all imaginable Demonstrations of joy, by discharing of Guns, ringing of Bells, bon-fires, illuminations, Fireworks, &c. and for a Fortnight nothing but Feasting. Three days ere the K. of *Spain* Arrived the Princess (Daughter of the K. of *Portugal*) designed to be his Queen, Dyed; and that loss like to made up by her Sister, some two years younger. Seven Grandees of *Spain* (besides those he brought with him) came to him upon his Arrival, who informed him that all places would submit to him assoon as he appeared. The English and Dutch Forces were about 12 thousand. The King of *Portugal* had 15. thousand, and daily leavying of New Forces: Upon his Arrival he sent the Forces to the Fronteers, reserving a few Companies for guard of his own Person to the Army, whither he designed to March that Week, that Capt. *Elson* came away & then directly for *Marid*. Upon the Fleets Arrival in *Lisbon*, consisting of about 22 Sail of Men of War, and about 300 Transport Ships: A Dutch Privateer being chased by 5 Sail of Men of War, informed Admiral *Rook* of it,

Printers' Terms

CARRIAGE — The part of the printing press that held a movable plank, on top of which was fastened the coffin.

CASE — The shallow partitioned boxes that held the printer's type.

CHASE — The large metal frame into which type was locked into pages for printing.

COFFIN — Located on the carriage, this was the part of the press that held the form of type.

COMPOSING STICK — The hand frame in which the type was set into words and sentences.

FLAT-BED PRESS — A press that held the type on a flat, horizontal frame, or bed.

FONT — A complete collection of metal type characters in one size and style.

FORM — The locked-up type in the chase, to be printed into pages.

FRISKET — A light frame hinged to the tympan.

GALLEY — The metal tray into which the set type was transferred when the composer's stick was full.

HEAD — The crossbar on the press from which the screw was hung.

HOSE — The box which enclosed the screw as it passed through the till.

IMPRESSION — The inked likeness of the type on the paper.

LETTERPRESS — The method of printing by pressing a sheet of paper against inked type.

LOWER CASE — The lower part of the type case, which held the small letters; hence, the term "lower case" for small letters.

MOVABLE TYPE — Single metal letters that could be combined and recombined into any words wanted by the printer.

PLATEN — A four-inch-thick piece of hardwood attached to the bottom of the screw on the printing press.

PROOF — The inked impression of the type in the galley. From this, corrections were made.

SCREW — The part of the press that lowered the platen which applied pressure to the paper and inked form, and so made the final printed impression.

SET — To put type into a composing stick, to form words and sentences.

SHEET-FED PRESS — A press on which sheets of paper were fed, one at a time, to be printed.

STONE — The large, flat surface — formerly made of stone — on which the forms were made up.

TILL — The crossbar on the press, through which the screw passed.

TYPE — The single metal letters of the alphabet which the compositor combined into words for printing.

TYPE FOUNDRY — The shop where metal type was made.

TYMPAN — The tightly fitted frame over which parchment was stretched. The tympan was hinged to the coffin.

UPPER CASE — The upper part of the type case, in which the capital letters were kept; hence, the term "upper case" for capital letters.

Some Colonial American Printers

ADAMS, JAMES	Wilmington, Delaware	(1761)*
BRADFORD, WILLIAM	Philadelphia, Pennsylvania	(1685)
	New York, New York	(1693)
DAVIS, JAMES	Newbern, North Carolina	(1749)
DAYE, STEPHEN	Cambridge, Massachusetts	(1639)
FOSTER, JOHN	Boston, Massachusetts	(1675)
FOWLE, DANIEL	Portsmouth, New Hampshire	(1756)
FRANKLIN, BENJAMIN	Philadelphia, Pennsylvania	(1730)
GREEN, SAMUEL	Cambridge, Massachusetts	(1649)
HASSELBACH, NICHOLAS	Baltimore, Maryland	(1765)
JOHNSON, MARMADUKE	Cambridge, Massachusetts	(1665)
	Boston, Massachusetts	(1674)
JOHNSTON, JAMES	Savannah, Georgia	(1762)
NUTHEAD, WILLIAM	St. Mary's City, Maryland	(1685)
PARKER, JAMES	Woodbridge, New Jersey	(1754)
PARKS, WILLIAM	Williamsburg, Virginia	(1730)
PHILLIPS, ELEAZER	Charleston, South Carolina	(1731)
RIND, WILLIAM	Williamsburg, Virginia	(1766)
SHORT, THOMAS	New London, Connecticut	(1709)
TIMOTHY, LEWIS	Charleston, South Carolina	(1733)

The date refers to the year in which these printers opened their shops

Index

Artist Leonard Everett Fisher says this of his books on early American craft workers: "I chose to write and illustrate a group of books on colonial American craftsmen because I know of no other time in our history when the aspirations of the people were so clearly expressed by their extraordinary craftsmanship. They were artists in every sense of the word. Their skill was a matter of profound and lengthy training. They applied themselves with energy and care. Their attitude was always one of pride in their singular ability and individualism. They were deliberate workmen who exercised such great control over their ideas, tools, and materials that they created one-of-a-kind objects that could not be recreated. The craftsman was master of his creations.

"I want my children to know this. I want their friends to know this. It is a most meaningful part of their history."

Mr. Fisher is a graduate of Yale Art School, where he was awarded the Weir Prize, the Winchester Fellowship, and an appointment as Assistant in Design Theory. Well known as an artist and an illustrator of children's books, as well as an author, his outstanding graphic work has been recognized by the American Institute of Graphic Arts in its exhibits of Outstanding Textbooks and Outstanding Children's Books.

The text of this book has been composed on the linotype in Caslon 137. This face is derived from the great oldstyle cut by William Caslon of London in the early eighteenth century. Caslon types were used widely by American printers during the colonial period and even today it is considered to be "the finest vehicle for the conveyance of English speech that the art of the punch-cutter has yet devised."

Natural Norwood Offset paper
supplied by Tileston & Hollingsworth Company, Boston

Composed by Lettick Typografic, Bridgeport

Printed by The Moffa Press, Inc., New York

Bound by H. Wolff Book Manufacturing Company, Inc., New York

DESIGNED BY BERNARD KLEIN